Frédéric Delalot

washingtonias and zoetropes 3

KDP Editions

Desire for change, crowd...

Entire panel of daydreams, inspiration

By chance, the past still existed...

Between the blinds, this theater...

Period of pace...

Nascent holiday rapprochements

In spacious detours

The opposite of things

All this...

Sometimes electronic delusions

Towers, illusions...

Indulge in this moment...

Become at leisure...

Outside, walk...

As a new approach

Attraction of these moments...

Below the bitumen...

Crazy embraces of suns...

Hypnotics, and we had peace

Desire to be reborn...

Warmth of possibilities...

Ah! we'd see you again...

Original snippets of happiness

The rest of the stories sprang up

Running after the moment...

Space, ephemeral hours...

Reveries, Tuscan cypresses

Memories...

On azure field, pine trees...

Driven by a force, an era...

With our continents...

In the most perfect night...

Sequence making machine

Fragments of translucent prints

The energy of steps, overflights...

Strolling between the eyes of the trees...

The dawn had seemed immense...

And we could see the city

Or inner courtyards

Solid stone walls...

All this was temporary...

Autumn had its attractions

Its interconnected colors

Desire for change, crowd

Under the palm trees and villas...

Remote boats, hyperpoles...

Thick stone walls, like a refuge...

Inaccessible, the trees of Phillips Square...

Crowns, stars in the city of water...

Fresh, all at once, systematic repetition

Very old sharing apps

From photos, vast underground cities

Entire panel of daydreams, inspiration

Indefinable, Christmas would not be long in coming

Abstruse ribbons...

The curious beauty

Appearances...

Transported us...

Then little by little the day rose...

In order to get to the other side...

Cities, North American atmosphere

Guaranteed, fuzzy ground of habit...

Feeling like a real individual...

From those times, even a feeling

By chance, the past still existed

Ancestors, oblique signs, round...

The rhythm of the present was a powerful force

Cabbage flowers, suns, Greek crosses...

Fed up with the air of intuitions...

For a long time, Volcom t-shirt, lying down...

Shutters closed, a few steps on the balcony

Top of the mountain, perhaps...

That we had invented this course...

We could see the city, inner courtyards.

Lying down, satisfied...

Unfulfilled, routine...

Maintain consistency

American, scorching

A story, first evening

House of La Loco...

A friend had convinced me...

To try Saint-Jean-de-Monts

Between the blinds, this theater...

Unlimited powers, planet, exploration

Televisions hanging on the walls...

Had retransmitted snippets, reality...

Each time this frozen island, red and gold

Winter had arrived

Completely renovated

Period of pace...

Seductresses, positions

Mind-blowing ships...

Embarking eras

We had this path...

It was jumping out of the mists.

Huge squares of entire troops

In the middle of the posters of the square...

Some indistinct sledges, benches

Under trees, gushing with pride

Nothing else happens, surely...

That a mysterious stay of thought...

Rapprochement of nascent holidays...

Our slow mirages, the atmosphere, were leaving

I saw glimmers...

In the trees...

Years had passed...

We weren't there yet

Thirsty for the taste of the desert...

Until the sudden relief...

They had soaked up the air of flight...

Lifting the paperwork of dreams.

Possibilities, mutual happiness...

Spinning from the depths of the ages...

To what end, common stirring

Start again, go out...

We had noticed

In spacious detours

I swallowed a kind of mixture...

Composed of the codes of reality...

Suspended from this boom, movements.

I perceived, shortly after

The gleaming tracks...

In the shape of a sun...

The decorative aisles...

The opposite of things

The sustained aromas...

Implausible stories

On the sea, bright...

The posters peeled off...

Columns, our moments...

Indifference, reassuring...

And bohemians, in the past.

Some happiness...

Inner continent...

Invisible until then...

Chance, discovering

Limitations and reason

All this...

Have peace...

Hope...

Longer...

That I would not have imagined

Check if I was equipped

A lighthouse transformed...

The color...

Days...

Strength of a procession

Uninterrupted...

The boats...

And the world...

Seemed far away

Hopes of time...

Deeper love

Feeling of serenity

Sometimes electronic delusions

Resistance, parsimony...

Over a very long period of time.

Happiness, look...

There was a silence...

Soothing, transparent...

Whose travelers adorned themselves

Plausible sail...

Some electrons

Here and there, isolated...

In nothingness...

Indigo, in the middle...

Towers, illusions...

Contrasts, carefree

At the edge of the expanses.

New Quebec...

We had been thought...

Until we fell asleep...

Custodians of happiness

Merits...

Reasonable...

Meet and forget

Dishes, mini-casseroles...

A certain magic was working...

Indulge in this moment...

Attraction, dancing on Les Cactus

At La Loco, it was far from all that

The Psalms had saved him

And books everywhere...

Embraced each other, on the ground...

Tiny elegance...

Acting on matter

Learning...

Always love yourself...

At night, energy

From our thoughts...

Connected us...

Become at leisure...

Like maps

Postal...

Illusions

Tacit agreement

Of all...

To be modified...

Renaissance...

In the world...

Outside, walking

From our silhouettes

Nature...

Armored campaigns...

Like that, full of life...

Don't change my appearance anymore.

And don't get old anymore...

You escape from yourself

La, la, la, la, la...

Indian resemblance...

This time, she was coming...

In white, accessible...

As a new approach

Of a classic style...

Chamomile, village...

In the city...

Crossing a forest...

Latino, hotel room

And she was on the verge of enjoyment...

With a word or a look...

Asian Light Column...

Only accessible to swimming.

Object of desire...

Wall of Angels...

Sifted with mirages

Ah! only see the sea

Suggestions of outfits...

Or fantasies...

Dreams, unbeatable mirages

Galaxies would merge

Attraction of these moments.

New scopes...

New roads...

Absorbed by the Sun

Perfect isolations...

Carved slates...

Below the bitumen...

Which was meandering, sighs...

With ether landscapes

There, isolated...

In nothingness...

Epilogue...

From an era.

Minute details of the silences...

Remote boats, rather machine

To make sequences...

Without brakes, without format...

Immediate love...

Provocative transition...

Crazy embraces of suns

Orgiiacs, crumpled sheets

The pleasure...

Collective...

Had diluted...

This certainty

Suddenly exhilarating...

You've always been free...

The intense story of a yesterday...

Of feelings, had fainted.

Her back, a tattoo...

At that time, I was wearing

Almost a decade...

See you again...

Drift of the senses

Book of emotions...

Gravitations...

Planets were engines

Hypnotics, and we had peace...

You were driving away

I don't know...

Where you were going...

We smiled at each other...

I could see them...

Revived beauties

Desire to be reborn

Instant, blue sky

Want to explore...

A few hours...

Secret life, things...

That we hadn't said to each other.

Happy face...

Our bodies embraced

Blottis, in Andorra

Or nowhere...

Drinking in the evening in the summer...

Of our loves...

Warmth of possibilities

Constantly renewed

A lighthouse, the port...

Initially unknown...

You still love her...

Salty morning from the sea

Happiness...

Perfect...

In these places

Those summers...

Ah! we'd see you again...

Possible abundance of meaning

I will always love you...

Magnetic nights

Maybe not...

I don't know...

There, feel the air...

Beneficial, our attractions

Eternity of embraces...

To behold, to your soul is ecstasy

Original snippets of happiness...

Slow transformation of beings...

And things, blue ink...

You can't write anything

Race of details...

Spiral feel...

Of a wandering order...

From an improvised party...

Surely from a pontoon...

Subtle apparitions...

Devoid of chains.

By the beauty of what is

Growing dose of unreality...

By memory, of causes...

As a result, this moment...

The rest of the stories sprang up...

Plot of minute coincidences...

Always admirable, contrasting...

Mirror of our aphrodisiac thoughts

I remembered being old

Very old, sitting on a bench...

Hacienda, world in itself, ideas...

Travels, thoughts of the moment...

Or memories

Collusion

Spaces...

Sailboats...

Entrenchment of eras...

Shared dailies, columns

Maverick crowds...

Perceiving emotion...

Strength to understand, to opt ...

The rest of the world seems distant

Almost unreal, yesterday...

Running after the moment

Plots of stories...

Floating by the way...

Yesterday, local residents, dreamers...

Our souls tempted, ardor

Studying short nights...

Drift and Bastille, later

Getting some fresh air towards the museum...

Orsay, distant azure...

Space, ephemeral hours...

Atmospheres, black trees...

Highs, electronic music

The road to Paris...

It was no time...

Yesterday, informal...

Culminating mornings

In a gargote...

Going to Béziers...

Like chanted words...

Months flown away, the courses...

Known, the jubilation, and these pedestrians

The carved words, the rushes...

Described wide circles...

Things were going by themselves...

Daydreams, Cypresses from Tuscany...

In the evening of Georgetown, so many alcoves

The energy of the deepest youth

In front of Notre-Dame...

By taking the time to drink...

The currents...

Beneficial landscape...

Discover the impossible

The quality of the nothings...

Search for these agreements

The immensity...

Memories

At birth...

Waves, episodes

Drifts of the hashes...

Travels...

Pieces...

No desire to give in

To the machines...

The insomniac ocean...

Bohemians from elsewhere...

Lighthouses, Hispanic waves

On azure field, pine trees...

The days were lost in fusion...

There was a fishing port, a massif...

Abandon the engines, change scenery

But no readings...

The sea, back to school, distance and epilogue...

More paths, big rooms

After, leave, musical conditions...

A park, fields, alternations...

The wind was rising, fragrant skies

The impression of falling in love...

Driven by a force, an era...

How many possible moments...

Much later

Back and forth...

Between the two shores

How many friends...

Snapshots of our micro-epochs...

Those days are gone, all elsewhere

Lightness, changes in the moment

Hopes, snow at dawn...

Late, Mount Royal

Go to the park...

With our continents

Random crossings...

Interior light, music

Places, turning endlessly...

Change...

From post...

Hypnotic.

And that's it, writing in the night...

In the most perfect night...

Through time and space

Getting to other levels...

Fantastic chandelier...

Clouds of memories...

Of towers, amalgam...

Which starts to take

Somewhere reviewed...

Relevant designs...

Colors in the universal

Behind the Illusion...

At each age its parade

Simultaneous requirements...

Can we say...

That there is a beginning...

The time comes, rather...

Machine for making sequences...

Long avenues opposite, coherence

Really, can we read the chance...

Later, go even further...

Risk aversion, price of the ounce...

Quiet, I didn't want to rush anything

Through the parks, the streets of moorings...

Faded pathways

With this time...

Capture a portion

Infinite cycles...

Stop a little...

Make sense...

In the middle of the waves

Local bazaars, sun side...

There was like an elegance...

Fragments of translucent prints

Then the street, art gallery...

Unmissable turrets...

Yielding to the heavens of dreams.

Intentions that surround us

Moving foreground...

Perfect weather variations...

The energy of steps, overflights

Silver beam lights

Juxtapositions, expectations...

Surely regenerative liquor

Miniature of joy, of summer...

Intoxicated medals

Sublime movements...

Oblique pleasures...

Multiple colors...

Hairy philosophers on zinc...

Prophetic paintings, trying to sail...

At the detours of July, we had known

By chance, very concrete shores...

Material hot paints

How many frolics, curves...

Elongated legs, lizards...

Happiness, at night...

Strolling between the eyes of the trees...

Voices of oaristys, meanwhile...

World of artifacts, sometimes silence...

And land of a glance, posted in Atlantis

However, as we move forward

I saw our desire...

All logic...

At that time...

14

Open Book, in addition to this era

The dawn had seemed immense...

Series of sequences, wills

And minutes surfers

Nuances of the century...

Coincidences...

What a possibility this world...

Would it have, at the heart of the senses...

Describe the universe, the platforms.

At night, he would stop near a property...

Urban adventures, through the breach...

The horizon armed its cavales, the future...

Would have its revival coronation, its peaceful reflections

I saw the essence of the rounds...

The sublime elsewhere, overlooking...

A vertiginous cove, randomly...

Libraries, next to fountains

Merry-go-round...

Roman river...

Photographs...

Wasted hours.

Hopes, possession and time...

Games, primordial drunkenness...

Departures, there, fashionable...

I had left the hours their speed

Spheres, stay young in the meantime...

Resort to our trips, to these dances...

Bizarre creatures again, so strange

We were walking in the streets...

We were looking at the youth

Drunkenness, rounds, outside

Automatic, profane pleasure

And principalities...

Would be used for reunion...

Alcoves with a passion for the streets...

The world went on, confusing

Sifted with fortuitous mirages...

15

Suite, makeup, getaways...

Also slimy potions...

Served in grapefruits

From our car, in the open air...

Flots, fashionable exiles of her youth...

Aesthetics, I heard the tamers

Whimsical, books...

Disparate library

On the other side of the spectrum...

Alcohol from trips, Atlantic...

The pylons of reality partitioned...

There was no place at the lost hour...

Cities, ephemeral, fragile palpitations

The bravest were travelling...

I knew some nymphs...

Of an unforgettable kind, characters...

Who give the music colors

Waterfalls of Oberkampf, precious city...

Torrid, behind the fountains of materials

There was a shortcut, alternative, European

Collective memory of geniuses, rhythms...

Of the rejoicing, the fabric...

Boldness, new exaltation

Immensely deliberate...

Filming, we started

Caresses...

In the middle of the empire...

Sun, golden...

Long lull

Latitudes...

Different...

Realize...

Something

Timely place, visual data...

Temporal routes would please

At their vibration, the osmosis fluid...

Giants, on this sphere...

16

Enigmatic fireworks ride...

Fleeting bridges, positions of each...

Recharged caverns, adorned with trophies

Where fountains sprang up

Orders from the planet...

Incomprehensible words...

Just a few good times

Some hypotheses in their minds...

Maybe we're getting attached...

To this story, this exterior

By not preventing anything

Things to flourish...

Which were deserts...

For having gone through time...

Intact, in a powerful momentum

Ancient knowledge...

Chance, immanent force...

In this sublime nature...

We crossed the space...

By a transversal era, shortened

Many times, like our alcoves...

Complicities snatched from bizarre flight..

That we find temporary, attractive ...

The silences had her voice, primordial

Framed photography, fountain, Capitol

And the passion against me, somewhat...

Stammered sentences, wandering caravan

At the edge, trotted in our minds...

Stunning pleasure, almost unreal...

Bareback, elsewhere...

Proximity, almost

Foolish worshippers

Awakened to beauty...

Things, living things

We would be magnetized

Mezzanines of lofts...

Statues in a square.

Crazy races, half-closed blinds...

Unbeatable dreams, yesterday, all that

Gold, primal air, night scenes

Also crossed

Roll of impulses...

Inaccessible...

At anchor points

Was it necessary to understand

The differences in time...

Nothing disturbed this landscape

The bond of enjoyment...

We had to observe the message...

Immediate, on the terrace...

And I was thinking about the cavales...

Surprising paintings...

Field, pearl brush

In the back seat...

I was catching stones...

For a moment of balance...

Youth, boats of a jubilation...

The heat occupied us with happiness.

I admit it, to this call of all time ...

By wealth, grains of plots...

We were driving unbridled, out of the rows

Era of linen, alcohols, models...

Motivations in the eyes...

Crowds, through the windows...

Or the paths, the changes...

Could we rebel, claim a place

Far from reality...

Leaning trees...

Sun licking

Near the tans...

Other achievements...

Picturesque forebodings

Could we be...

More disconcerting...

Drunkenness of the cities...

Carefree perfume...

Hugs, twists and turns

Evaded, on the back of the boxes

Volutes of the mind...

Escape into the middle

Intertwined rebirths...

I gave myself the time to undertake...

To appreciate the atmosphere, décor of rays.

Thus, everyone was interested in pleasing themselves

Inventing virtual homes...

We don't see much of the aircraft carriers...

Immediate vial, party, absorptions...

Repeated, I had found a car...

Open, with poncho seats, abandoned...

From the tunnel escaped the vehicles...

A few trinkets, again, a few touches

I saw these excerpts...

In the immediate embrace...

Quiet power...

Whose origin we did not suspect.

In the excitement...

Discovery...

We were looking at each other

Faded lanes...

Impregnable rock...

In the past, to be born...

Gigantic paintings...

Waiting gateways

Nothing happens, apparently

But everything remembers...

From a silence, nothing happens...

On the other hand, than a mysterious stay

Thought, like a conversation

Lamp sheltered from the wind, enjoyments

Particles and dust in space...

And this time, you can't write anything...

As a new approach

Attraction of these moments...

Which was meandering, sighs...

Without brakes, without format

Drift of the senses...

I don't know...

Those summers...

Magnetic nights

Subtle apparitions.

Mirror of our aphrodisiac thoughts...

The rest of the world seems far away...

Space, ephemeral hours...

The energy of the deepest youth

Beneficial landscape...

Bohemians from elsewhere...

The feeling of falling in love

Places, turning endlessly

Getting to other levels...

Really, can we read the chance

Yielding to the heavens of dreams...

Miniature of joy, of summer...

Material hot paints...

And surfer minutes...

I saw the essence of the rounds...

I had left the hours their speed

Suite, makeup, getaways...

There was no place at the lost hour

Boldness, new exaltation...

Just a few good times...

By a transversal era, shortened...

Complicities snatched from bizarre flight

The unbeatable dreams, yesterday, all that...

The heat occupied us with happiness

Era of linen, alcohols, models...

Intertwined rebirths...

From the tunnel escaped the vehicles

Gigantic paintings...